The Importance of A Father

By:

Pastor Sally Edwards

AiON MULTIMEDIA
"The Word is Eternal" Isaiah 40:8

Printed in the United States of America

Published by Aion Multimedia
20118 N 67th Ave
Suite 300-446
Glendale AZ 85308
www.aionmultimedia.com

ISBN: 978-0-9976046-5-8

TABLE OF CONTENTS

Proverbs 22:6 (NKJV)

[6]Train up a child in the way he should go,
And when he is old he will not depart from it.

INTRODUCTION

BEST DAD IN THE UNIVERSE

I BELIEVE MY TWO DADS ARE THE GREATEST IN THE ENTIRE UNIVERSE. I HAVE TWO DADS. ONE IS MY HEAVENLY FATHER, GOD, THE OTHER IS IVAN. ALTHOUGH I HAVE ANOTHER DAD, HE CHOOSES NOT TO BE IN MY LIFE. I FORGIVE HIM BECAUSE THAT IS WHAT GOD WOULD WANT ME TO DO. IN THIS ESSAY, I WILL BE WRITING ABOUT MY EARTHLY DAD AND WHY HE IS THE BEST DAD IN THE UNIVERSE.

MY HEAVENLY FATHER BLESSED ME WITH A DAD HERE ON EARTH WHICH IS IVAN FIGUEROA. MY DAD, IVAN, FIRST CAME INTO MY LIFE WHEN I WAS EIGHT MONTHS OLD. IVAN HAS BEEN THERE FOR ME EVER SINCE. THROUGH THE UPS AND DOWNS, HE'S THERE TO USE THE PADDLE ON ME EVEN THOUGH I STILL DON'T THINK I NEED IT. HE IS THERE TO HUG ME WHEN I'M SAD OR DON'T FEEL WELL. HE IS THERE EVEN WHEN I'M TRYING TO BE MAD. HE DOES HIS BEST TO GET ME LAUGHING. I LOVE HIM SO MUCH BECAUSE HE TREATS ME AS HIS OWN.

MY DAD IS THE BEST DAD BECAUSE HE WORKS HARD TO PROVIDE FOR ME. HE GETS UP BEFORE THE SUN COMES UP AND SOME DAYS HE DOESN'T COME HOME UNTIL WAY AFTER THE SUN HAS COME DOWN. MY DAD IS THE BEST DAD BECAUSE HE CAN BE GOOFY...

...IF WE'RE LUCKY, SOMETIMES, HE'LL SING A SPANISH LOVE SONG IN SPANISH WHICH MAKES MY MOMMA SMILE. HE ALWAYS MAKES THE "BOMB.COM" SALSA AND GUACAMOLE.

LAST, BUT NOT LEAST, MY DAD IS THE BEST IN THE UNIVERSE BECAUSE HE PUTS GOD FIRST. MY DAD TAKES ALL OF US TO CHURCH SO WE CAN LEARN AND GROW MORE IN CHRIST. SO THAT WE CAN BECOME WHAT GOD HAS PLANNED FOR US AND STAY HUNGRY FOR GOD. THAT IS WHY I THINK MY DAD IS THE BEST DAD IN THE WHOLE UNIVERSE AND DESERVES TO WIN TODAY ON FATHER'S DAY.

CHEALSIE, AGE 14

FATHER'S DAY ESSAY 2016

INTRODUCTION

Dictionary.com lists one definition of "father" as a man who exercises parental care over other persons ("Father"). Just like Chealsie was saying in her essay, parental care doesn't necessarily mean that they are your natural children. Many of you reading this little book may have grown up in a situation like Chealsie's. Some may have had another parent step in and take over as a father. Some may not. It's possible that your natural father didn't really make a conscious choice not to be in your life. It may be that no one ever taught him how to be a daddy. He just didn't know what to do or how important his role was in your life. As a pastor, I'm very proud of Chealsie and all those like her who forgive their absent natural fathers. I want to encourage anyone that has an absent father to always leave that door open. At some point in your life, he may want to be a part of it.

But let's be honest. Fathers don't have to live somewhere else to be absent from their children's lives. It's not right for us to ignore our children and to not take care of them. But some people simply do not have those tools or skills because they were not taught or shown when they were growing up how to act, how to be a father, how to love their children, and how to discipline them. And if you don't have skills, then you don't have those skills. I mean, they don't just automatically pop into your head one day. How many of you were handed an owner's manual when you gave birth? Kids aren't cars – they don't come with bumper to bumper manuals. There are some good parenting resources out there, but I guarantee you, they don't cover everything.

So it is up to us as parents to, *"Train up a child in the way that they should go: and when they are old they will not depart from it" (Proverbs 22:6, KJV).* Look at that carefully. It says we have to train them up in the way they should go. It doesn't mean that they are going to always walk the straight and narrow. That doesn't mean they are always going to do everything right. But it does mean that you have the hope of seeing them, at some point, doing and saying the right thing. It will come back to them.

CHAPTER 1 – BE WHAT THEY NEED WHEN THEY'RE YOUNG

> *⁶ For unto us a child is born, unto us a son is given: and the government shall be upon his shoulder: and his name shall be called **Wonderful**, **Counsellor**, **The Mighty God**, **The Everlasting Father**, **The Prince of Peace**. (Isaiah 9:6, King James Version, emphasis mine)*

Isaiah 9:6 lists five names of God. Each one means something different to every person who reads this verse. This list doesn't contain every name of God. He's also known by El Shaddai[1] and Elohim[2]. Those names also meant something very special to each one of the tribes, or people that used them because when they called Him El Shaddai, "God Almighty", He had just delivered them[3].

---

[1] Genesis 17:1

[2] Genesis 1:1

[3] Exodus 6:1-3

When they called Him Elohim, the "God That is with Us[4]", they felt His presence in the midst of their trial and tribulation. With every one of these names, when the people called out to Him, they called out to what they needed and what they saw Him being for them. In many ways a natural father is like that.

One time we needed to put some blinds up in my husband's office. So, my good, loving husband, Reverend Ricky, was in there putting them up while Megan and I were in the living room. All of a sudden it sounded like something was just shoved across the floor in there. I sat and thought, "What is he shoving around in there?"

But Megan got up to investigate, "Mom! Dad's lying on his back in the middle of the floor."

Now, usually I laugh when this stuff happens, but it looked pretty serious. "Are you OK?" I asked.

"I will be in a minute," he grunted.

Turns out, since he didn't know where the step ladder was at that moment, he just pulled his rolling desk chair out from underneath his desk to stand on. He had to

---

[4] Deuteronomy 31:6 and Joshua 1:9

put some pressure on the blind to get it to pop in, and when he did that, the rolling chair went flying out beneath his feet in the opposite direction. I'm just thankful he didn't go through the window. You know, he laid there a good long time before he got up. He's tough as boot leather so I knew he was hurt. The next morning he had a sore hand, a sore elbow, and a sore hip. But you see, even though he got hurt, he was being what I needed – a window blind installer.

When the kids were little and they were fighting, he would be the referee. When he was there I was very thankful because I didn't have to do it all. I stayed home most of the time when the kids were little. I did have to work some, but either way, I appreciated it so much when he came home and helped with the kids.

Fathers, I know you feel like you come home from a long, hard day's work and all you want to do is sit down and watch TV, or read, or whatever it is you do to relax, and get your mind off a long day's work. But just take a minute and be a daddy. Give Mom some relief. Be a daddy and let your child know that you're not just a bill payer because when they get to be 16 and you're just the bill payer, you can't get mad at them if they walk up to you with their hand out. When all you've ever been is the bill payer, you can't expect to now be the one that is instructing them and teaching them. You have to start that stuff when they are little. You can't wait until they are 17 or 18 years old and be the disciplinarian.

I'm going to tell you right now. Those little kids who are 2 and 3 years old that are running your life don't suddenly stop and line up when they get to be teenagers. If your life is centered on your kids' wants, needs, and desires, then you are making a huge mistake because kids need to learn to adapt to every situation in life – not have everyone adapting to them. If we make everything so comfortable and easy for them that they don't have to use any restraint, judgment, wisdom, or knowledge when they are little bitty, then guess what? They won't know how to do it when they get to be 16, 18, or 20 years old.

I'm a bail bondsman, and I'm telling you, I'm bonding people out of jail who are 40 and 50 years old and their parents are still co-signing for them. It breaks my heart. I've told those parents, "You need to make them grow up." But for some of them, unfortunately, it's probably too late. They're not going to grow up because they're too old, and Momma and Daddy are still bailing them out of everything.

We have to play these scripts out. If you are only living to take care of your children right now, what's going to happen when your children leave? Trust me. They will find somebody. They will fall in love and they will leave. Are you going to have to start all over with your wife? Or are you planning to look for a new one now that you aren't "tied" to them anymore? This is real. Divorce happens all the time after the kids leave home because people think that way. It is a direct result of not doing what was necessary when their children were little to make the marriage relationship a priority.

CHAPTER 2 – A STRONG NATION BEGINS WITH STRONG FATHERS

Do you know how a child forms their opinion of right and wrong? The grown-ups in their lives tell them. Mom and Dad tell them. That's how they form their opinions. The kind of father we need in the world today is one who not only pays the bills, but who also boldly tells the children, "Hey, this is not good. This is not right."

If you see something that is totally crazy and don't discuss it with your kids, then they think, "Huh? Dad's OK with that? It must be OK," or even, "Mom's OK with that? OK, it's no big deal. I can do it too." Without saying a word, you just told them how to form an opinion about that issue. You just showed them an example of what was OK.

Whenever I see something that is wrong, I try to talk to my kids about it. Now, hear my heart, I'm not trying to judge people for everything they do. I understand that I am not the sheriff of the Body of Christ, so I don't tell my kids, "We need to go tell them and straighten them out." No! It's not my job to straighten everybody else out. My job is to form my kids according to the WORD of God – to

THE IMPORTANCE OF FATHERS

teach my kids to think according to God's will, His ways, and His commandments. I want my kids to know that they aren't going to be blessed if they do that same thing.

You know, if you ask most teenagers these days, "What are the Ten Commandments[5]?" don't be surprised if most of them don't have a clue what you are talking about. You don't see them anywhere anymore. They've been taken down from the courthouses and all the public places, so you don't see them anymore. If you don't go over stuff like that and read it to your children, they won't have any idea what's right and wrong. (See Appendix 2 for a copy.)

Let's take a look at how important these commandments, or statutes, are to God:

> *[1]Now therefore hearken, O Israel, unto the statutes and unto the judgments, which I teach you, for to do them, that ye may live, and go in and possess the land which the LORD God of your fathers giveth you.*
>
> *[2] **Ye shall not add unto the word which I command you, neither shall ye diminish ought from it**,*

> *that ye may keep the
> commandments of the LORD
> your God which I command
> you. (Deuteronomy 4:1-2, KJV,
> emphasis mine)*

In verse two, God is telling us, "Don't add anything
to the WORD of God and don't omit anything from it.

> *3 Your eyes have seen what the
> LORD did because of Baalpeor:
> for all the men that followed
> Baalpeor, the LORD thy God
> hath destroyed them from
> among you.*
>
> *4 But ye that did cleave unto the
> LORD your God are alive every
> one of you this day.*
>
> *5 Behold, I have taught you
> statutes and judgments, even as
> the LORD my God commanded
> me, that ye should do so in the
> land whither ye go to possess it.*
>
> *6 Keep therefore and do them;
> for this is your wisdom and your
> understanding in the sight of the
> nations, which shall hear all
> these statutes, and say, Surely
> this great nation is a wise and
> understanding people.*

⁷ For what nation is there so great, who hath God so nigh unto them, as the LORD our God is in all things that we call upon him for?

⁸ And what nation is there so great, that hath statutes and judgments so righteous as all this law, which I set before you this day?

*⁹ Only take heed to thyself, and keep thy soul diligently, lest thou forget the things which thine eyes have seen, and lest they depart from thy heart all the days of thy life: but **teach them thy sons, and thy sons' sons;** (Deuteronomy 4:3-9, KJV, emphasis mine)*

In other words, when we teach God's commands – God's statutes – they are not only what's going to keep you going as a family, but they are going to keep us going as a community. They are going to keep us going as a nation. He's talking to a whole bunch of people right here. But I'm telling you, it starts at home with you and how you teach your kids and your grandkids.

It starts at home with your children – how they view things, how they see things. If you don't know what the Ten Commandments are look them up and read them in Appendix 2 or in your own Bible. Read them to your children. Then explain to them that we keep them because we want to live in the land of promise. We want to live in that land that He gave us in Deuteronomy 4:1. We want to be the people that possess the things that God has given us. The only way to do that is by keeping His statutes.

After we figured that out, we no longer told our kids that they could grow up and be anything they wanted to be. We quit telling them that because so many people are being what *they* want to be instead of what God has called them to be. This generation needs men and women willing to teach their kids that God has a plan and a purpose specifically for them. He's got something called into their life for a special time and a special place and the only way they're going to get there is by following His plan – His statutes – His commandments.

Look, there are millionaires out there that are ungodly. They are living horrible lives. Everything looks good on the outside, but they're miserable on the inside and have no peace. I'm going to tell you right now, I'd rather live a peaceable life. I want to go to sleep at night when I lay down in the bed. I don't want to be there worrying if this is going to happen or if that is going to happen or who's going to be on top tomorrow. When I go to bed, I want to be able to go to sleep. And when I do the plan of God, I can, because I've done everything He's told me to do.

Our responsibility as parents is to teach our kids the WORD of God, to teach them to honor God, to teach them to go to church, to teach them to fellowship with people of the same faith. We don't have to be robots, but we do have to be like-minded people because if you've got somebody fighting you all the time on what you believe, you're likely to give up some of your beliefs. If somebody keeps saying, "You don't have to worry about that. You know, God really didn't mean that." You could slip and be led astray. I know people, men of God, that because of an errant thought or something that happened in their life, changed their whole belief system. Over time, as more and more men and women changed their belief systems, the whole fabric of the nation has gradually changed. This is the stuff the parenting books don't teach you.

CHAPTER 3 – FATHERS SHOULD BE PROTECTORS

A father is to protect – not only physically but emotionally. At our church in Woodville, we had a young, preteen girl who wanted to get up and sing a special song. Her grandmother was a singer at the church, had a great voice, and said that the little girl wanted to sing. Since it was our last Sunday as pastors there, I agreed. So this happy little girl gets up on the stage and everything was fine until she looked out into the congregation. I saw this fear come over her. I mean it was like she just lost everything – it all left her.

I told her, "Just put your hands over your eyes. It'll be fine." I could imagine what she was thinking because I've been there myself. I didn't want her to sit down because so many times, if they sit down out of fear, they never get back up and try again. So, she covered her eyes and the music started but she didn't start singing.

That's when a man walked up. I thought he was her daddy, but actually, he was her grandpa. He stood directly in front of her. Very gently and very nicely he said, "Put the microphone to your mouth and sing." He stood between her and the congregation so all she could see was him. I was so impressed.

When she finished singing, it was my turn to speak to the church, "This daddy…"

"Granddaddy," he corrected.

"This granddaddy cares enough to protect her and save her," I exhorted the congregation. You see, we need daddies that save their little girls. We need daddies that save their boys. We need daddies that will go out of their way, and even if they look silly, will do it anyway for their kids, because that means something to them. That little girl was probably able to get back up and sing again because of what her grandpa did for her that day. If he hadn't done that for her, it probably would have turned into something that would've tormented her for the rest of her life. In my eyes, he saved that little girl that day. That's what fathers are for. Jesus saved us and He's the ultimate Father.

Fathers uphold. That means they give support against an opponent ("Uphold"). The best way to uphold something is by the WORD. We uphold against the enemy. We keep him off by the WORD of God. So when our kids aren't listening to us – when they aren't doing what we say

– we still have prayers that we can pray for them. We still have the things that we can say according to the WORD of God. This is how we uphold our kids against the enemy.

Part of being your children's protector is teaching them by example how to live peaceable lives. You mostly form your children's thoughts and actions by your lifestyle, so make sure you are living right before them. More is caught than taught, so we have to live our lives right before them and *then* we teach them to do the same.

Lately, this word peaceable is meaning a lot to me because I see so many people in torment. I'm not against medication. But the sheer number of people that are on anti-depressants and other medications just to allow them to sleep at night is overwhelming. If they had a peaceable place or position, they would be able to do that, but the devil is tormenting people. He wants to get them so torn up and stirred up that they can't live their life.

> [17] *But **the wisdom that is from above** is first pure, then peaceable, gentle, and easy to be intreated, full of mercy and good fruits, without partiality, and without hypocrisy. (James 3:17, KJV, emphasis mine)*

We must learn to operate in the wisdom that is from above.

> [11] Now **no chastening for the present seemeth to be joyous, but grievous**: *nevertheless afterward* **it yieldeth the peaceable fruit of righteousness** *unto them which are exercised thereby. (Hebrews 12:11, KJV, emphasis mine)*

Pretty much every child around the world is going to agree that no chastising is pleasant. None of them want a whipping. But that discipline, that spanking, yields the peaceable fruit of righteousness. It helps them understand that they need to be in right standing with God. When you are in right standing with God, you can live a peaceable life.

CHAPTER 4 – PRACTICAL PARENTING TOPICS

Part of being what your kids need is being a teacher. Don't worry, I'm not talking about math and science here. I'm talking about character. There are too many areas to discuss them all in this booklet. However, I would like to hit on a few that will make a significant impact on your children's lives. If you start early, teaching them in these areas, the benefits will spill over into other areas of their lives as well.

SOCIAL ETIQUETTE

Fathers, teach your kids how to act in public. Don't say, "I'm not taking my kids anywhere with me because they just act crazy! Somebody has to come to my house and watch them." No! You start teaching them how to act in public from the time they are little. If they stay home all the time, how will they learn? You'll end up with a 16 or 17-year-old that doesn't know how to act in public. Teach them when they are little.

I know what I'm talking about. I've had a strong-willed child. In fact, I've had just about every "type" child there is: strong-willed, mellow, easy, and etc. Strong-willed children take more time. But, I was the grown-up! I was going to win. I did and he is a preacher of the Gospel today. That is not to say that there weren't times I wanted to step in between my husband and him. But I knew I couldn't because it was a man thing and he needed to learn. My husband always said, "If you're going to act like one [a man], you're going to get treated like one."

COMMON COURTESY

Teach your children how to be courteous – especially to the elderly, infirm, or pregnant ladies. I can't tell you how many times, when traveling, we've seen teenagers lying across two or three chairs at the airport when an older man or woman walks up. As an adult, I can tell they're most likely exhausted, but there they are standing and trying to hang on to their luggage. Yet the kid never gets up. I look at the parents and think, "Make your kids get up. Make them respect elders. Make them see that they need to honor older people." But they don't. Most of the time, the parents have got their headphones on and they're looking at their iPads and the kids have theirs – they are all oblivious to what's going on around them. Fathers, kids don't figure these things out on their own. They have to be taught.

I remember one time there was an incident with a pregnant woman. She was huge and having a very hard time. There were these teenage boys just sitting there looking at her like, "Lady, you're in my way." I don't know about you guys, but these things just make me furious. Unfortunately, there was no daddy there to say, "Hey, get up and give her a seat." So guess how they are probably going to treat their wife. You see, this is what a lot of people don't realize, the way a young man treats the women around him is generally how he will treat his wife when he is older.

APPROPRIATE ATTIRE

Teach your kids how to dress. When they are little bitty kids, they are learning every day. Therefore, if we want them to dress modestly when they are teenagers and older, then they need to learn to dress modestly when they are little. Don't wait. Besides, there are all kinds of perverts out there everywhere just waiting to look at little kids. Think about this for just a minute: if you thought you were dressing your child up every day for a pedophile to get his kicks, how would that make you feel? We have to be wiser and more careful than the predators to protect our families. It is our responsibility as parents.

FINANCIAL MANAGEMENT

It is never too early to start teaching your children about money. You can't wait until they are 18 and say, "OK, you're out the door." Fathers, you have a very important part in all this. Start them young with small jobs, which are extra from their household chores, and pay them a little something. Then teach them to tithe, to save, and to manage their spending. If they grow up doing this, it will be natural for them to continue doing it when they get their first part-time job. Teach them to have a bank account and to reconcile it. Teach them about the dangers of credit cards and mismanaged debt. Teach them about investing. Did you know Dave Ramsey, the founder of Financial Peace University for adults has similar courses for children and high school students[6]?

These are our responsibilities as parents. If you teach them while they are young, you will save them a world of hurt in the future. Fathers are to nourish their children. Nourish means to promote growth. That's not limited to physical growth, but spiritual as well. Promote growth in your children. Always help them to see things from God's perspective.

[6] http://www.daveramsey.com/store/kids-teens/cYouth.html

APPENDIX 1 – SPIRITUAL SALVATION

In Luke 15, Jesus explained to a group of people, some who went to church and some who didn't, what it was like for God when one of His lost children came home to Him. First Jesus compared the lost person to sheep that got away from the flock. Even though the shepherd had 99 other sheep, he still went after that one and carried him back home rejoicing (Luke 15:4-7). To God, we are like that one sheep that went astray. He sent Jesus, our Great Shepherd, to go find us and bring us back home. Then look what He said:

> *7 I say to you that likewise there will be more joy in heaven over one sinner who repents than over ninety-nine just persons who need no repentance. (Luke 15:7, NKJV)*

Next, Jesus compared the lost person to a coin that a woman loses. Though she has nine others, she cleans and searches her house diligently until she finds it. Again she rejoices (Luke 15:8-9). Again, look at God's perspective:

> *10 Likewise, I say to you, there is joy in the presence of the angels*

of God over one sinner who repents. (Luke 15:10, NKJV)

But the most important comparison Jesus makes is in the Parable of the Lost Son. You see, this son decides he's tired of living at home with his father. He wants to go off and make his fortune. So he asks for his portion of the inheritance and takes off. For a while, life seems great. He has all kinds of fun and friends – living high on the hog. But as soon as his money runs out, he finds himself living with the hogs and so hungry their food actually looks good to him. Sin always takes you farther than you want to go and keeps you longer than you want to stay. Finally, he decides the servants in his father's house have it better than he does. Maybe if he goes back home he can ask his father to take him back – not as a son, but as a servant (Luke 15:11-19). But look what happened:

> [20] *"And he arose and came to his father. But when he was still a great way off, his father saw him and had compassion, and ran and fell on his neck and kissed him.* [21] *And the son said to him, 'Father, I have sinned against heaven and in your sight, and am no longer worthy to be called your son.'*

> *22 "But the father said to his servants, 'Bring out the best robe and put it on him, and put a ring on his hand and sandals on his feet. 23 And bring the fatted calf here and kill it, and let us eat and be merry; 24 for this my son was dead and is alive again; he was lost and is found.' And they began to be merry. (Luke 15:20-24, NKJV)*

Dear one, you are so precious to God that He sent Jesus to go after you even though you strayed from the flock. You are like that precious coin. He won't stop until He has you in His hand also. But most of all, you were created as his child, and He's waiting for you to come home to Him.

Most people who've been around church any length of time know John 3:16, "*For God so loved the world that He gave His only begotten Son, that whoever believes in Him should not perish but have everlasting life*" (NKJV). But few know the next verse:

> *17 For God did not send His Son into the world to condemn the world, but that the world*

through Him might be saved.
(John 3:17, NKJV)

What does it take to be saved? It's easy. We recognize that we have sinned and fallen short of God's plan. Then we confess with our mouth that Jesus is Lord and believe in our heart:

> [23] *for all have sinned and fall short of the glory of God,*
> *(Romans 3:23, NKJV)*

> [9] *that if you confess with your mouth the Lord Jesus and believe in your heart that God has raised Him from the dead, you will be saved.* [10] *For with the heart one believes unto righteousness, and with the mouth confession is made unto salvation.   (Romans 10:9-10, NKJV)*

If you are ready to be found – to come home – then pray this prayer aloud:

> *"Father, I'm lost and ready to come home. Father, I believe you sent Jesus into the world to save me. Jesus, I believe You are who You say You are – the Son of God. I believe You died on the cross for my sins and*

I believe God raised You from the dead in victory. I know I have sinned and I repent. I ask your forgiveness. Please come into my heart, save me, and be The LORD of my life. I am yours and you are mine.

Thank You! Amen"

If you just prayed that prayer, we are rejoicing with Heaven right now. Tell someone. Call a Christian friend, call a local church, or even write our ministry office and let us know so we can be praying for you. It is important that you confess your new salvation to someone else to strengthen your faith. Then, be sure to get into a strong Bible-believing church this Sunday. There's a whole lot more great stuff God has in store for you[7].

Pastor Sally Edwards
Ricky Edwards Ministries
P.O. Box 621
Pawnee, OK 74058

---

[7] Jeremiah 29:11

Appendix 2 – Ten Commandments

¹And God spoke all these words, saying:

*² "I am the L*ORD *your God, who brought you out of the land of Egypt, out of the house of bondage.*

³ "You shall have no other gods before Me.

*⁴ "You shall not make for yourself a carved image—any likeness of anything that is in heaven above, or that is in the earth beneath, or that is in the water under the earth; ⁵ you shall not bow down to them nor serve them. For I, the L*ORD *your God, am a jealous God, visiting the iniquity of the fathers upon the children to the third and fourth generations of those who hate Me, ⁶ but showing mercy to thousands, to those who love Me and keep My commandments.*

*⁷ "You shall not take the name of the L*ORD *your God in vain, for the L*ORD *will not hold him guiltless who takes His name in vain.*

*⁸ "Remember the Sabbath day, to keep it holy. ⁹ Six days you shall labor and do all your work, ¹⁰ but the seventh day is the Sabbath of the L*ORD *your God. In it you shall do no work: you, nor your son, nor your daughter, nor your male servant, nor your female servant, nor your cattle, nor your stranger who is within your gates. ¹¹ For in six days the L*ORD *made the heavens and the earth, the sea, and all that is in them, and rested the seventh day. Therefore the L*ORD *blessed the Sabbath day and hallowed it.*

*¹² "Honor your father and your mother, that your days may be long upon the land which the L*ORD *your God is giving you.*

¹³ "You shall not murder.

[14] *"You shall not commit adultery.*

[15] *"You shall not steal.*

[16] *"You shall not bear false witness against your neighbor.*

[17] *"You shall not covet your neighbor's house; you shall not covet your neighbor's wife, nor his male servant, nor his female servant, nor his ox, nor his donkey, nor anything that is your neighbor's." (Exodus 20:1-17, NKJV)*

BIBLIOGRAPHY

"Father." n.d. *Dictionary.com Unabridged.* Random House, Inc. 2016 August 18. <http://www.dictionary.com/browse/father?s=t>.

"Holy Bible, King James Version." 1987. *Bible Gateway.* Ed. Public Domain. Online Bible. 15 September 2015. <https://www.biblegateway.com/versions/King-James-Version-KJV-Bible/>.

New King James Version. Nashville: Thomas Nelson - HarperCollins Christian Publishing, Inc., 1982. web-based on BibleGateway.com. 11 May 2016. <https://www.biblegateway.com/versions/New-King-James-Version-NKJV-Bible/#booklist>.

"Uphold." 2016. *Dictionary.com Unabridged.* Random House, Inc. 26 August 2016. <Dictionary.com http://www.dictionary.com/browse/uphold>.

www.ingramcontent.com/pod-product-compliance
Lightning Source LLC
Chambersburg PA
CBHW071653040426
42452CB00009B/1853